Love Re-membered

Resources for a House Eucharist

❖❖❖❖❖❖❖❖❖❖❖❖❖❖❖❖❖❖❖❖❖❖❖❖❖❖❖❖❖❖

JIM COTTER

CAIRNS PUBLICATIONS · SHEFFIELD
in association with
ARTHUR JAMES LTD · EVESHAM
1996

© by Jim Cotter, 1996
ISBN 0 85305 347 2

First published 1996

Cairns Publications
47 Firth Park Avenue, Sheffield, s5 6HF

Arthur James Ltd
70 Cross Oak Road, Berkhamsted, Herts, HP4 3HZ

Further copies of this book
and other Cairns Publications
can be obtained from Arthur James Ltd

Printed by J. W. Northend Ltd
Clyde Road, Sheffield s8 OTZ

Contents

For Colin
For Sarah
with gratitude

Preface

OVER the past seven years, quietly, and without fuss, I have been hosting a House Eucharist in my home in Sheffield. I have not wanted to found a sect or to gather a small cliquish Sunday congregation. (In fact one of the delights has been that there have almost always been new faces at each celebration.) I suppose it has been a case of conducting an experiment in a laboratory, nothing wildly eccentric but with a wordsmith's concern for the language and metaphors of prayer, and a 'fool's' understanding of how many people are hurt or bewildered by the churches' ways of worship, with its assumptions of a patriarchal and hierarchical God. I am thinking of both the Sunday norm and the apparently friendly but often authoritarian house churches.

There comes a time when the results of an experiment have to be made available in the public arena. Hence this book. It may be that some who read it would like to have the texts themselves, uncluttered by the commentary and in a form that is easy to use in an act of worship. They are available from myself at 47 Firth Park Avenue, Sheffield, s5 6HF. For a fee of £10 you will receive a set on A4 sheets, printed on both sides, together with copyright permission to make up to twenty-four further copies. I hope this is an easy and fair way of coping with a minor but vexed question of conscience.

However, I do hope that any group might have a copy of this book to hand. For it seeks to give the contexts along with the texts, in the conviction that different sizes and shapes of rooms and buildings, along with the different cultures of the people present, affect and are affected by the actual words used. We are living in a time of pluralism which no longer holds to one text for all circumstances, but which has to ask the questions and find some answers to the problems of boundaries, to the need for common values that can hold the 'Body' together.

In my turn I need to acknowledge my thanks to Stainer and Bell Ltd for permission to reprint the words of two hymns by

Brian Wren, 'Here hangs a man discarded' (1975, 1995) and 'Christ is risen! Shout Hosanna!' (1986). Their copyright holds throughout the world except in the USA, Canada, Australia, and New Zealand.

I am grateful to Alan and Elin Dodson for the design of the cover of this book, Alan for the typography and Elin for the sketch of the front of my house.

My thanks also go to Bishop John V. Taylor, some of whose phrases I have used from his book *The Go-Between God*. He graciously suggests that such material is our common property in Christ—which makes me feel somewhat mean in asking for fees. My only excuse is that the labourer is worthy of some reward, at least until the cash flow is less erratic. (I can always dream!) I am grateful to David Lunn, Bishop of Sheffield, for his Foreword. He taught me Doctrine at theological college thirty years ago, and I remember his preaching about the Church offering an open Book and hosting an open Table.

JIM COTTER
Sheffield, June 1996

Foreword

THIS is a book to be read slowly and prayerfully–it has a three-fold importance.

Firstly, it can open the eyes (and the heart) of those, like myself, who have become routinely accustomed to the traditional words in a traditional building, to the rich inner meaning of what we are about when we 'break the bread'. Such readers will be astonished, infuriated, and occasionally moved to murmur, "You must be joking!" But as they read they will find that this book brings profound illumination. We learn what the Eucharist is for and we get sudden insights into what those first gatherings at the Lord's Table must have been like. And the Cotter 'midrashes' (or re-workings) of the traditional forms and prayers do lead us to deeper understanding of the purpose and meaning of all the words we use in common prayer. Anyone who is called to lead worship should "read, mark, learn, and inwardly digest" chapter two, "The waiter, host, and guide": it will result in repentance, a new beginning, and a transformation of much of the ordinary worship of our churches.

Secondly, we live in an age of liturgical change, and sometimes we seem to have handed over the worship of the Church to the liturgical experts: historical correctness can outbid pastoral need. Here we do begin with the need of the worshipper. In that bout of liturgical revision which will lead the Church of England to a new Prayer Book in 2000, we need to be able to apply the Cotter test of devotional usefulness to all that is produced.

And thirdly of course the book will be a 'vade mecum' to those who find themselves close to that piece of ground on which Jim Cotter stands. Perhaps curiously I find myself pointed in the way of that domestic holiness that meant so much to our Victorian ancestors. Does the Cotter 'Spare Room' point to a revival of family and household prayers?

DAVID LUNN
Sheffield, June 1996

1
A spare room: the context of place

POUND for pound (or euro for euro, or grand for grand), you can rent or buy more domestic space in or near the inner city than in the suburbs or the city centre, let alone the national park a few miles away. You may then have the 'luxury' of a surplus room, over and above the requirements of domesticity, work, and guests, a room that could earn you some income if you let it out. Or...?

Perhaps, though, you live in those suburbs. You moved there some years ago because you needed more room for your growing family. Now that the children have grown up and left home, should you move again, to a smaller house? Or...?

Perhaps you have inherited a flat in the city centre from your father. It has four rooms, and, living alone, you calculate that you need only three. Does the fourth idle away, half full of junk? Or...?

I am fortunate to have such a luxury: an empty room. How to use it? I could let it out–the thought of the extra cash is temp-. ting. But there is a deeper desire, born of my experience of living on the edge of the Church, concerned that the language and style of worship have been captured by images and practices of hierarchical and patriarchal power and status. I am uneasy about those forbidding west doors of cathedrals which are opened only for processions of the 'grand' on 'grand' occasions.

Power is so easily misused. How might I use mine? Ordained in, but not these days paid a stipend by, the Church of England, I find myself enabling celebrations of the Eucharist on a small scale, for groups on retreat, at conferences, and–in that surplus empty room. Yes, I do have power–licensed by a bishop to mini-ster in 'his' diocese; backed by nearly thirty years' experience of caretaking (i.e. taking care of) liturgical celebrations; not wishing to found a sect, and therefore wanting to be 'in communion' with other cells and communities and churches; owning, for the time being, sufficient space to gather a dozen or two people at the same time; employing a skill as a wordsmith in crafting most

I

of the prayers printed in this book; having the last word in the furnishing of the room.

The scale may be smaller than that of a cathedral (though not that of a chapel in a cathedral); the imagery used may be more about compassion and friendship than about dominance and lordship; I may not find it appropriate to wear ecclesiastical costume; but I still have to ask, How can the power entrusted to me, and claimed by me, be used to 'serve communion', to enable each person's (including my own) sense of eternal worth, tactfully to encourage our openness to one another and to God, to unfold our finely balanced needs for both comfort and challenge? And what, in practice, and in detail, have I found myself doing over a period of seven years in this 'laboratory'?

I begin with the 'luxury', the *given* space at the top of a house. How do you help an empty room become a 'Spirit-place', a 'praying place', a 'breathing space'? Better, perhaps, a place where the Spirit and people can breathe, either alone or in a group?

The particular room in question is on the second floor of an Edwardian semi-detached house, some two and a half miles north-north-east of the centre of the city of Sheffield. It measures approximately seventeen and a half feet in length, thirteen and a half in width. It is small enough for one person not to feel overwhelmed by too much space, large enough for twenty people not to feel crushed. There is a light fawn fitted carpet, and the walls and ceiling are painted white. This is the basic decor of the rest of the house, linking the rooms together so that the praying place doesn't immediately feel very different from any of the other rooms. (On one of the walls there is a patch of damp, the cause of which more than one expert has been unable to diagnose. Ah well, nothing in this life is perfect...) Here is a ground plan of the room, on the scale of a quarter of an inch to a foot. (I still can't think in decimals where measurements are concerned!)

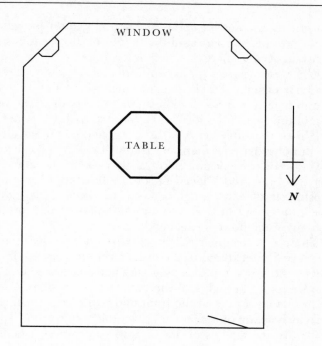

The room has the feel of an attic. It is about eight feet high in the middle, with a flat ceiling five and a half feet wide, but there are eaves which slope down to the wide walls, which are themselves only four and a half feet above the floor. Where the eaves meet the ceiling proper, there are two beams, one on each side and running the length of the room. Behind them are two sets of two lights, again on each side (i.e. eight lamps in all), and these are operated from four dimmer switches by the door.

If you sit facing the window, your eye will miss the tubular bells (they have a rich resonance) suspended from one of the beams at the rear left of the room, the mini-CD and tape player tucked in the corner by the door, and a slide projector on a shelf half way up the centre of the back wall (and above the radiator). Your eye might catch the two mini-speakers above the window, and the rolled up projection screen, but these do not intrude. On the whole, you won't be distracted by the mechanics of sounds and sights that may be used as ways into thought and prayer. I hope that the technology is appropriate not only to my budget but also to the size of the room and the nature of the occasions in it: no excess of decibels here.

What you will see, some two-thirds of the way to the window, is an oak octagonal table, one foot high, three and three-quarters feet in length and width. The shape reflects the 'bay' at the far end of the room (the sides of the bay are wall, not window). The height of the table reflects the insistence of the eaves that the 'centre of gravity' of the room is low. If twenty people stand you have a crowded cocktail party; if they sit or kneel, the sense of space is preserved. Placed on the table is an octagonal slab of Westmorland slate, rough around the edge, a inch and a half thick, the upper surface smooth and hollowed out so that it can contain water, flowers, and candle.

There is a 'tryptich' of three sash windows giving a view of much of Sheffield and of the distant Pennine moors–houses and trees, hospitals and parks, industries and sports stadium. At night you see only the lights of the city, stationary ones illuminating streets, moving ones at the front and rear of cars: you can easily imagine you are on a plane that is coming in to land.

One of the aspects of prayer is to place oneself, or for us together to place ourselves, at the intersection of Spirit and stuff, articulating the joy and bearing the pain of the interaction. If the prayer of the inner journey becomes intense, there are blinds that can be drawn down over the windows to keep awareness of the city dimmed for a while. If the prayer is helped by works of the imagination, the rolled up screen above the window can be lowered for the projection of pictures–a kind of temporary stained glass.

Rainbow colours sometimes move over the walls and carpet, when the sun shines through a crystal suspended two-thirds of the way down the top section of the middle window. Beneath it, a quarter of the way down the lower section, is suspended a cross of inward-pointing nails, with a minute hole in the middle, a 'narrow gate' that challenges a spiritual slimming. (Perish the kind of cross that is mere 'sign', neither recalling the horror of crucifixion, nor communicating the deeper symbolism that can evoke our engagement and response: we are too easily lulled by the jewelled processional crosses given to cathedrals by wealthy patrons, or the casual pendant, or the cross that has, to Christian shame, made so many Jewish people cower.)

At the left hand end of the window ledge are a couple of small cacti, at the right hand end, a small cairn. In the middle is a photograph of planet earth from space, with a night light in front of it, contained in a translucent porcelain cup of duck-egg size. Two further lights illuminate a picture of a clown (the left hand bay), and the Rublev ikon of the Trinity (the right hand bay), each light resting on a small half-octagonal table, whose surface is a foot and a half above floor level–the same height as the window ledge.

So the room is not empty, but feels spacious. The 'fixtures' are few. Most objects are easily portable. Chairs, stools, books, crockery, bread, and a bottle of wine are kept on the landing outside, to be brought in for particular occasions. What is not used is removed afterwards. It is a bit like the use of a kitchen by a community. If everything is cleared away after use, the space is welcoming to the next person who wants to prepare a meal or make a drink.

Because there is room only for an 'extended family' at most, where each can at least be aware of everybody else, and because the original design of the room lowers the 'centre of gravity' towards the floor, there is no room for hierarchies and high altars (or pulpits), and perhaps the lower half of the body can feel more welcomed than it usually does in churches.

The 'chapel' is somewhat whimsically dedicated to the Advent (a place of waiting and watching), the Holy Fool (the Feast of Fools on the first of April is the best patronal festival anyone could want–hence the picture [ikon?] of the clown), and the Desert Fox (the fennec fox is a small mammal with disproportionally large ears for picking up the faintest sounds in the desert: an encourager of the careful alert listening that is part of prayer, not least the listening to the earth and the city, to one another, and to the Silence that is beyond the words).

The various objects in the room may or may not have the power to move the imagination of those who pray there. If not, they remain empty of meaning to anyone but myself, and in time they will become like those ornaments rich with association for the person who displays them, but rather pathetic when their owner dies and their story vanishes with them. But I hope the objects can become, at least for some, aids to imaginative prayer. Yes, they are a personal choice, but I trust not idiosyncratic or individualistic. Each of them has a story or a resonance: people and places are brought by association into the place of prayer. The small cairn is built of pieces of Millstone Grit, the sandstone of the local 'Dark Peak' District, which underlies the garden. The slate bowl comes from the Lake District, a mere fragment of Norman Nicholson's 'twenty thousand feet of solid Cumberland'. The tables are the only objects specifically designed with the 'givenness' of the space in mind: they were made by a local carpenter from oak, the species that I am fairly sure originally clothed the land on which the house is built. (That reminds me to add a codicil to my will, to provide for the planting of a few oak trees when I've gone. And I take comfort from the actions of a friend of mine who goes around the open spaces nearby sowing acorns.)

Millstone Grit, Westmorland Slate, the wood of an oak tree: none of them is far removed from the flesh and blood bodies that move in and out of the 'Spirit place'. In the Eucharist they may be focused on bread and wine, but no material thing is left behind in the yearning for transformation. Neither is commerce and trade, even if I can't remember the brand name of the emulsion paint that coats the walls—and I hope the carpet was made in West Yorkshire, though all I know is that it came via Allied Carpets.

People come crowding in along with the things—the potter friend who made the containers for the night lights, and those who have brought or sent gifts (not necessarily with the room in mind)—the picture of the clown, the cacti, the Rublev ikon, the crystal, the cross of nails, the photograph of the earth, the current candle (in the shape of a yellow open petal for the Eastertide in which I am writing this). They bring to mind the givers and their various 'worlds', and are samples of that close web of which we are all a part—a retired wing commander and probation officer who is now doing his bit to help the campaign to remove the ban on gay men and lesbian women serving in the Armed Forces; an associate vicar who works particularly on issues of sexuality and spirituality, and explores how women and men *together* may minister more creatively in the churches; a social worker who is rather more new-agey than I am, but whose crystal casts those patterns of rainbow delight (the rainbow which these days has become a sign of the glory of racial and sexual diversity); a dancer who, well into her seventies, did the splits as a gesture of exultation and offering during an Easter celebration; and two or three from years ago whose names my head has forgotten but whom I trust my heart still holds dear.

Others have contributed in several ways to the texts used at celebrations of the Eucharist. Their place will be acknowledged later in this book. Together they are 'present' to those who are present in the flesh. Perhaps we are just a few of that interlocking network more commonly known as the communion of (lesser) saints.

That more or less describes the 'spare' room, and fills in some of the background. It is of course a unique place, irreplaceable. That is not to say that it should be enshrined, preserved beyond its living day. It is temporary, provisional–as is its instigator. But the opportunity, and the questions to bring to that opportunity, are certainly available much more widely than we usually think. If the combination of spices in the dish I have prepared is unique to me, the basic ingredients are waiting for others–to use with their own flavours. Is there possibly an imaginative (and persuasive!) cathedral canon reading this who could re-arrange a musty side chapel for celebrations of the Eucharist, no better or worse in style than any other (even, I am reluctant to admit, those grand occasions), its focus nearer the earth than above the already 'high' altar?

That brings me to the actual contribution that I usually make at such celebrations in the Chapel of the Advent, the Holy Fool, and the Desert Fox. How do I make it? What is the word? Celebrant, president, host, waiter, servant of communion?

2
The waiter, host, and guide: the context of leadership

THE important tasks are done in the hour before people arrive and in the hour after they have gone. Again, it is a matter of paying attention to, taking care of detail, so that there is as little as possible to impede the flow of love between us and between us and God. Here then is my check list:

Is the slice of bread cut from the loaf (fresh and fibre rich, of course!) and ready for bringing to the table?

Is the bottle of wine in a convenient place? Also the plate and the cup? (The wine is an ordinary port, and the crockery has been made by the same potter who made the containers for the night lights, and in the same materials.)

Are the two copies of the Bible in place on the table, with readings marked, for the convenience of the volunteers who don't yet know they will respond to the request before we start, Will two people read for us?

Are the service books in a pile on the stairs, ready for each person to take a copy? (Another detail: they are A4 display books, each with twelve plastic covers to protect the sheets of paper and to make the turning of pages almost silent. There are the additional advantages of being able to replace single sheets, to add a sheet with any extra material needed for a special occasion, and to put the page *numbers* on the plastic covers rather than on the paper.)

Are the prayer stools (three of them) and the conventional stools (twelve of them, made in Sheffield at the centre for those who are blind) on the landing for each to take one? Some choose to sit on the floor. And is there a hard-backed chair nearby in case someone comes who needs it by reason of physical infirmity (or inflexibility!)

If slides, tapes, or compact discs are to be used, are they in place, so that only the press of a button is required at the appropriate time? Pauses during the service should be meant, and not

9

be a cause of anxiety and fuss because care has not been taken beforehand.

Is there anything needed that is particular to this occasion today?

Does a list of names of people to be brought into our prayers need to be in place?

Moving to the kitchen, preparing for the refreshments afterwards, are the two kettles filled with water? Are the mugs and spoons in place, and the jug of milk and bowl of sugar, the teapot and the tea, the coffee jar and the decaff., the cake and biscuits?

This all sounds boring, and so it may be. But routines can be satisfying as well. Without this attention to detail, you can't murmur a contented, All is prepared. (Caution: If it happens that something has been forgotten, I hope I have the grace to laugh and stay relaxed when the realization dawns.)

The responsibility can of course be shared. Others can be involved in the preparation. It is a help if someone nips downstairs quickly at the end of the celebration to switch the kettles on—or put pizzas in the oven if there is to be a shared meal. The tasks of clearing up afterwards can involve others too—the endlessly repeated washing, drying, and putting away. It is the very last of those that this particular host insists on doing himself when everyone else has gone: otherwise tea strainers and biscuits are lost for weeks. But I find I need to accept offers of help graciously, whilst both participating in the chores themselves, *and* keeping an eye on the well-being of the whole occasion.

What I find I do *not* need to do is to be the only or the dominant voice in the actual act of worship itself. As will become clear in the section of this book that gives the background to the texts used, some parts are said or sung by everyone together, while other passages are said by solo voices, each person in turn speaking a paragraph or two. All I need to do is lightly to 'conduct' if someone needs a nod who is unsure about starting to read. Once in a while the showman in me breaks through, but the unfolding of the Word is shared amongst us, with the opportunity for those who wish to comment on the readings from the Bible.

Where actions are concerned, as host/waiter I pour the wine, I break the bread, and I serve the first guest. Each in turn serves his or her neighbour, and at the end I am the last to receive. We say the words of remembrance ('institution') together, and, yes, I like to be 'in touch' at that moment with the physical stuff of the bread and I like to enfold the cup in my hands. I do this on behalf of the whole company, not by reason of exclusive power, but so as not to distance ourselves from the transformation of the material – our own flesh and blood bodies included. On occasion, however, after the words, "Do this to re-member me", we pass bread and cup round in silence, so that the hands of each can touch them.

I *think* this is, in one particular context, an authentic way of being in 'holy orders', doing the chores (the waiter/deacon), sacrificing pride of place even if I have the authority to preside that comes both from experience and from the community's approval (the host/presbyter-priest), and, greatly daring, guarding the good of the whole and connecting in principle with other 'communions' (the over-seer/bishop).

However, the chores come first and last. The host in Yeshua's communion gives up any status and waits at table and washes feet in the role of a slave woman. We need to give due emphasis to the *shock* of both 'slave' and 'woman' in the context of the society, both political and religious, of Yeshua's time. Gorgeous apparel becomes a very ambiguous sign. (Sigh – but I do so love a party and dressing up for it...) And the guide sits on a stool like everyone else. If you have a beautiful Jacobean chair in your church, put a cushion on it and lift that disabled member of the congregation on to it. Your discerning bishop will prefer a plain chair, and both will be more comfortable.

3

The words and the actions:
the texts and their contexts

WHEN guests arrive to meet round the 'open table' in the (at least temporarily) 'open house', they are, I hope, welcomed as courteously as would any churchwarden or steward in a church porch. But they are not immediately given a book, bewildered by a sheaf of papers, or shown to a pew. Coats find their way on to hooks, a nod is given in the direction of the loo, and the door is open to the living room in which we gather. Those who know one another can share news and strangers can find a welcome. There is a fire to warm us in winter (gas, not logs, I'm afraid, but at least the flames look cheerful).

When everybody has arrived we introduce ourselves to one another. A name is all that the shy are asked to give. But everyone has the opportunity to speak briefly of any concern or person that they bring with them—gratitude for a walk on a sunny spring day after a long grey winter, a cousin in hospital with cancer, a looming interview for a job, the cattle at the height of the BSE crisis. So we are able to take one another into the corporate prayer as we climb to the spare room, the breathing space. (By the way, asking each person to say their name is a tactful way of recalling that which has been embarrassingly forgotten.)

The sharing of concerns has recently led to an innovation. It must be that my early Methodist conscience was troubled by not having that one essential element of nonconformist worship —The Collection. A bowl in the hall now invites contributions to a charity close to the heart of one or two of those present.

So we move to the praying place, collecting a folder (and stool if wanted) and sitting in the shape of an approximate horseshoe. We gather almost but not quite round the octagonal table. The circle is not closed: we leave the window uncluttered so that we are open to the beyond—both of the city and of God. We keep

silence as we accommodate ourselves to the room and its atmosphere. Then the words and the actions begin.

What follows here is the order of service, section by section,
text first, then context

Approach

> Eternal Spirit, living God,
> in whom we live and move
> and have our being,
> all that we are, have been, and shall be
> is known to you,
> to the secrets of our hearts
> and all that rises to trouble us.
> Living Flame, burn into us,
> Cleansing Wind, blow through us
> Fountain of Water, well up within us,
> that we may love and praise
> in deed and in truth.

This opening prayer to the Spirit for honesty and truthfulness in
life and worship has its source in the Collect for Purity at the
beginning of Holy Communion in the Book of Common Prayer.
For convenience I reproduce it here:

"Almighty God, unto whom all hearts be open, all desires
known, and from whom no secrets are hid: Cleanse the thoughts
of our hearts by the inspiration of thy Holy Spirit, that we may
perfectly love thee, and worthily magnify thy holy Name;
through Christ our Lord."

Ah! The rhythms of the English language on the mouth and
pen of a sixteenth century wordsmith! There is beauty in the rise
and fall of the word-sounds, and I can find myself poised between awe and adoration of the beautiful mystery of God on the
one hand, and fascination and seduction by a magical power on
the other. That is one of the problems of well worn prayers: the
wrong kind of power, the illiterate dominated by the educated,
the peasant by the lord, and, so easily by association, the
cringing sinner dominated by a God whose velvet glove hides an
iron fist. It is the word 'Almighty' that gives the clue. It may well

have its roots in a notion of the powerful creative energy of God, but in English its associations are with absolute monarchs (or dictators, media moguls, and chairmen of multi-nationals). We have to tread very carefully. Too many of us, even with no direct contact with the 'powers that be' beyond tax forms and council tax demands, have felt power exercised *over against* us, by parents, teachers, bosses. More subtle, more hidden, less frequent is the power *shared with* others, let alone given away to others, empowering them to further their well-being. Only power infused with love and justice can do this.

Another clue is the word 'secrets'. With whom do you share the kind of secret that, once in the light, makes you vulnerable to shame or sarcasm, mockery or condemnation? You can do so only if you can trust the other not to use the information against you: a trusted friend is pure gold.

The picture of God with which we start should not even hint at a person who could intimidate us and make us cower in fear. But if we believe we are opening ourselves to the Presence in whom we *already* intimately live and move and have our being, then we can pray that the power of love and wisdom and guidance will empower us to words and actions of integrity and truth. Through drawing close to God, and God drawing close to us, in an act of worship we may find ourselves embodying that same love, wisdom, and guidance, and so showing forth the renewed image of God in us.

Elemental pictures of the Holy Spirit enrich the prayer – the flame of fire, the wind, the water, all of which shape and re-shape the stuff of earth and the matter of our bodily selves.

The prayer is for honesty, for open hearts and flesh, for transformation. Greatly daring and greatly trusting, we approach, in friendship, the Living Mystery of Wisdom and Love.

Recognition, Kyries, Forgiveness and Reconciliation, Peace

When we really open up to the truth of ourselves, we find that we are facing more than we bargained for. We realize that we are warped by illusion and the lie, we limp from harm inflicted by others and ourselves, we are wounded by our failures both to love others and to receive their love. We need 'open heart surgery' to clear the hardness that impedes the flow of love's lifeblood. Traditionally, this part of the Eucharist is called Confession and Absolution. I have used the titles 'Recognition' and 'Forgiveness and Reconciliation', by association less mechanical, less concerned with states of sin and status of power broker, more personal, dynamic, and restorative of relationships.

Recognition

Beloved and faithful Creator,
you formed us from the dust
in your image,
and you redeemed us
from sin and death
through the living,
dying, and rising
of the One who is
your very Word made flesh.
Through baptism
you accepted us,
cleansed us,
and gave us new life.
You called us
to your service and friendship.
But we have wounded your love,
and marred your image.
We have wandered far
in a land that is waste.

Silence

From all our corporate
and personal sins,
from those to which we are blind,
and from those
we cannot now remember,
we turn to you,
wounded God,
in repentance
and in trust.

Again, I can approach with trust and without fear the One who is my 'Beloved and faithful Creator', whose discerning judgment may well be sharp but is contained within a greater loving, unlike the condemning judge pronouncing sentence from the lofty heights of moral indignation.

The language used for 'sin' is that of 'wounding your love' 'marring your image' (the exact phrases used in the prayer are borrowed from one of the forms of Confession in the Alternative Service Book of the Church of England), and 'wandering in a wasteland'. There are many other phrases and images that could be used, in relation to both personal and corporate 'sins'. A community or congregation could well compile its own variations, some of them particular to its own experience and that of the village, town, or city around.

There is time for silent reflection on personal particularities, that which lies heaviest on our own hearts, and then turning towards a God who is not sleek, but wounded.

Kyries

> Kyrie Jesu Christe
> Huios Theou eleison

The Kyries have been used in a variety of ways in the Eucharist, for example as a congregational response in a sequence of intercessory prayers. Here they are deliberately placed within the process of telling the darker truths.

The Christian story has touched many languages and cultures, and those who gather to worship do well to remind themselves of that history, and of the ancestors of the faith with whom we belong in God. So a smattering of Greek and Latin, Hebrew and Aramaic, doesn't come amiss.

There is an advantage is saying or singing 'Kyrie' and 'eleison' rather than 'Lord' and 'mercy'. The associations of the words are richer in Greek than in English. The prayer 'Lord, have mercy' is not a terrified plea to be let off punishment by a stern judge who is reluctant to temper justice with mercy. That is the result of narrowing and legalizing the concept of judgment in Western Christian thought. 'Kyrie' translates the Hebrew 'Yahweh', which can be shortened to 'Yah', as in 'Hallelu*yah*', 'Praise *the*

Lord. 'Yah' is a basic word-sound, the 'Yes!', 'Ya!', energy of creative power, God's hoot of delight at the wonder and complexity of the universe. 'Eleison' is associated with an abundance of blessings of every kind.

So: sing it in Greek! Or, at least this: "Loving energetic Creator, pour blessings abundant upon us."

The text above uses an expanded form, that of the Jesus Prayer of the Orthodox tradition: "Lord Jesus Christ Son of God have mercy." It is a kind of mantra, and can be hummed while walking along a beach or round a park. At the House Eucharist we sing it three times to a simple melodic line.

Over the centuries, five parts of the Eucharist have traditionally been sung: Kyries, Gloria, Credo, Sanctus, and Agnus Dei. (That's five words in Latin already!) We follow that, in a variety of musical ways.

Forgiveness and Reconciliation

True love, divine love,
is sure and steady,
absorbing our hurt,
never deflected by it,
accepting tragedy
and redeeming it,
involved with us,
closer to us than breathing,
exposed and vulnerable
to everything we do.

True love, divine love,
gladly accepts the truths
of our hearts,
runs with delight
to embrace us,
favours us
at the banquet of joy.

Jesus Christ
embodied that love
and calls us

to embody it too.
To those who promised
to weave its pattern,
the Spirit was given,
to forgive
or withhold forgiveness,
to enable or defer
the forgiveness of God.

In the name of Christ,
aware of that gift of forgiveness,
seeking to embody the Gospel
of unconditional love,
with the voice of Christ
resonating within us,
let us say,
each to all,

I forgive you.

And let us hear
the word of Christ
to us, the Body of Christ,

I forgive you.

So let us be assured
that we are forgiven,
forgiven by Christ,
forgiven by our fellow-pilgrims,
released from all that hurts us.
Amen.
Thanks be to God.

This is considerably longer than the usual form of Absolution. Traditionally the form of Confession is longer. That is to get the proportion wrong. We should be focusing more on the love of God than on ourselves, paying more attention, sensing the pulse of forgiveness and reconciliation. So this prayer reminds us of the cost of forgiveness *and* the joy and delight with which God runs to welcome us to the banquet.

There is emphasis on our own participation in the process, the challenge to embody it in our own lives. The third section above is an attempt to express the dynamic realized truth of the gift of the Holy Spirit to the whole Church, the People of God: "If you forgive the sins of any, they are forgiven; if you retain the sins of any, they are retained." (John 20.23, RSV) It is an awesome thought, having the power to forgive, *and* having the power to withhold that forgiveness. *We* can defer the forgiveness of God, not out of ill will or a desire for revenge, but precisely because its dynamic cannot come into play without both the willingness to forgive *and* the repentance of recognition on the part of the one who needs forgiveness. So it is in this text that we are all invited to say the words "I forgive you": they are not the preserve of the host. With and in the Spirit of Christ, "with the voice of Christ resonating within us," hearing the word of Christ spoken to everyone, by everyone, we signal our desire to be caught up into a reconciliation that reaches deep within and far beyond us. And we proclaim the assurance of forgiveness and the release from the sting of our hurts. Only a small moment of course: much remains to be worked through in ourselves and our relationships. But there is nothing to bar us from the banquet. In any case the worst that can happen is that we exclude ourselves, and I suspect we do *that* only until we 'come to ourselves'. Then it seems as if the whole world changes—and perhaps it does. If you catch hints here of the Parable of the Prodigal Son, that is no coincidence. Remember the elder brother.

Peace

> Let us live together
> in the reconciliation
> wrought by God
> and in the Shalom
> God wills for the universe.

> The Shalom of God
> spread around you.
> The Peace of Christ
> be with you.

Spiritually and psychologically, this seems to me the most appropriate place to share a gesture of the Peace of Christ, the Shalom (another Hebrew word) of God. It is the moment that some dread and others relish. But it has nothing to do with reserve or ebullience of temperament. We need to be careful. This is not the time for a gesture that is dependent on how well we know the person we are greeting. Those who hug easily need to reflect on the reality that this excludes the shy and the stranger, and this is definitely *not* the moment to do that.

Yes, something needs to be *done*, some bodily sign given. But it needs to be one that acknowledges that it is the Peace of *Christ* that we share, a blessing I would wish on everybody, from those I am finding most difficult to be alongside to those who do not yet know that I find them exceedingly attractive.

So the gesture is formal, and the same for each person. We pass it round the room, one to the next, inviting everybody else to focus, in turn, on the one receiving the greeting, thus encouraging a more deeply aware 'communion'. This is one of the advantages of sitting in the shape of a horseshoe: nobody has to twist a neck to see somebody else. The touch is usually that of a typically formal English handclasp, though I personally favour the receiver placing his or her palms together and the giver placing his or her hands round the other, together with that slight bow of reverence which is the one saluting the divine within the other. I do believe that the touch is itself important: we greet one another as embodied beings, not as souls in danger from the corruptions of flesh.

Having been cautious at this point, I do have to add that the experience of 'communion', in all senses of the word, usually flows into humanly warmer greetings at the end!

Gloria

> Worship give to God most glorious—
> Peace to those who love God well—
> Adoration from God's people—
> Thankfulness our voices tell.

God, we bless you for your glory,
Full of light and truth and grace,
Word made flesh in Christ incarnate,
Shining through a human face.

Born in cave and killed on gibbet,
Outcast dying in disgrace,
Burned by fires of human hatred,
Raised by Love's fierce last embrace.

Jesus Christ our glorious Saviour,
Lamb who takes our sin away,
Lifted high in Love's enfolding,
For your mercy here we pray.

You alone are Love most holy,
You alone great deeds have done,
Intimate in God in glory,
In the Spirit, Three-in-One.

When there is a large congregation in church or cathedral, the service usually begins with a rousing hymn, perhaps in procession, with strong accompaniment from the organ, and trumpets on high festivals. By contrast, a House Eucharist can begin quietly, as has been described so far—silence at the beginning, a short silence in the middle of the Recognition, quietly sung Kyries, a whispered, gentle sharing of the Peace. But by the time the Peace is given and received there is a slight quickening of the heartbeat: a stronger voice is needed, and the Gloria is its expression.

A small company is not up to Schubert, nor even one of the modern settings that congregations can sing if given a good lead by a sensitive choir. Better a version in the form of a hymn with a tune that is familiar to most of those present. The metre is 87.87, and we usually sing the tune *Love Divine* by John Stainer: we have to give the much maligned Victorians their place in the story too!

The words 'glory' or 'glorious' appear in each verse except the middle one, where the mood darkens to remind us that true glory transforms rather than banishes pain and death. The glory is that of golden light, of translucence, of transfiguration. It is the glory that evokes wonder and adoration and love. It is not the glory of military or political might: there is no place here for the crown or for jewels, however prey to temptation Christian writers have been to use the symbols of earthly power and wealth to picture the glory of God. Of course all picture language falls short, and God is beyond our imaginative powers. But we can at least ask that poetry hint at the truth rather than obscure it.

Meeting the birth far from home, the death that of a disgraced outcast outside the city, the look of fiery hatred in human eyes, and overcoming them, is the fierce embrace of love, the enfolding of love, the intimacy of love—more powerful than any armed host of heaven.

Prayers, Readings, Reflections

These are all particular to the day. A sample of the material used on one occasion is given in chapter 4, for the Feast of Fools. Traditionally this is the Ministry of the Word, and I hope the more Protestant inclined of my readers will not be offended by only a few brief thoughts.

It seems to me important to see this part of the service as a whole. We recognize it by a prayer that relates to the theme of the day, by two or three readings from the Bible, one of them always being from the Gospels, and the 'breaking' of the Word, an interpretation in our own language, sometimes aided by pictures and music.

One part of this process is prepared beforehand, either by a particular choice for an unusual occasion or by reference to one of the lectionaries of the churches. And I will have selected and put in place a slide or a CD, or both—or neither. In practice, I do all this myself, but there is no reason why it shouldn't be a shared activity, and the better if it is so. The experts too can be called in to help, either from commentaries on the passages chosen or from your RE teacher or professor if there is one in the company. The presentation of the Word can weave picture and poem, music and reflection, in and out of the words of scripture. That can remind us that the readings themselves do not exist in 'holy' isolation: they reflect the concerns and experience of the writers and their communities who in times past sought to respond to the God who had been revealed to them, however partial their understanding of who God is and how God acts—and the implications for their lives.

Such a presentation does, however, have a drawback, even if it is the best way of breaking the Word when there is a large number of people. Those gathered in a room can more easily make their own contribution to the discerning of the Word. No one is of course obliged to speak, and it is not the place for an argument or discussion, but a variety of contributions, from questions to fresh insights and images and stories, can enrich everybody present. If the company falls silent, well, that gives time and space for quiet rumination, for that inward digesting recommended by the Collect for the Second Sunday in Advent in the Book of Common Prayer.

Personal admission: once in a while, the showman in me gets the upper hand, and I hold forth—though never for more than a few minutes! My responsibility is not to do all the 'breaking of the Word' but to encourage an atmosphere in which we can surprise one another with some fresh truth of God.

Credal Hymn

> Barely I believe yet truly,
> God is One and God is Three,
> God is Love and seen most fully
> Hanging from the wintry Tree.
>
> And I trust Creator Spirit
> In and through our common life
> Weaving threads all torn and broken,
> Shaping justice out of strife.
>
> And I cherish—with due patience -
> For the sake of God alone,
> Friends and strangers as one Body,
> And the Sacraments Christ's own.
>
> I embrace the Law of Loving,
> Dying to possessive need,
> Risen with Christ, though crushed by winepress,
> Into spacious glory breathed.

The response to the Breaking of the Word is an Affirmation of Faith. Usually, this is the Nicene Creed, dating from the first years after the political triumph of Christianity over the Roman Empire. It was an attempt to define orthodoxy over against the current heresies. It is not a full statement of belief to be set in stone for all time. It is probably not the credal statement that would be made by the synods of the churches today. More than thirty years ago I listened to a series of lectures on the New Testament given in the Divinity School in Cambridge by Charlie Moule. My only distinct memory now (alas the passing of the years) is the claim he made that the Nicene Creed's statement on the Holy Spirit is inadequate to the witness of the New Testament. It runs: "We believe in the Holy Spirit, the Lord, the giver of life, who proceeds from the Father and the Son. With the Father and the Son he is worshipped and glorified. He has spoken through the prophets." He went on to refer to what he thought was the key verse in the New Testament: "God has sent the Spirit of his Son into our hearts by which we cry, Abba, Father." (Galatians 4.6) This is an altogether more dynamic and intimate understanding than is implied by the more formal and elevated language of the Nicene Creed–the Holy Spirit as the energy by which we are brought through Christ into close touch with God.

So it is entirely traditional to work at new statements of faith, fresh unfoldings of what we have inherited. Indeed, this is what hymns have often done, one example being John Henry Newman's *Firmly I believe and truly*. I sang that hymn in Grace Cathedral in San Francisco in the autumn of 1986, and the following day I led an evening of meditation for those caring for people with HIV and AIDS. I suppose I was feeling angry at what came across to me as a triumphalist creed, from the days of British imperial self-confidence. '*Firmly* I believe' was too rock-solid a way of putting it when faced with the dilemmas and horrors of an epidemic, too easy, too glib. So my mind and imagination set to work, and began with the thought, '*Barely* I believe *yet* truly.'

We sing it to the tune with which Newman's hymn is usually associated in England, Shipston. It is a Warwickshire ballad, harmonized by Ralph Vaughan Williams. So it is that composers both unknown and famous are with us in the worship, part of the stream of endless song. But other melodies in 87.87 metre will of course serve just as well.

The first verse speaks of a suffering God who in Christ has AIDS. Crucifixion, with its pain, horror and shame, is centre stage in any attempt to justify the ways of God to the anguished.

The second verse recalls our experience of life as torn to shreds, but has a hint of hope that our common life will weave even the darkest threads into a pattern of justice, of relationships that have 'come right'.

The third verse acknowledges that the Church is not usually an encouraging place for gay and lesbian people to be openly a part of. It still seems hard for most Christians to recognize that the Body of Christ has AIDS, that indeed everybody on the planet today, as well as the earth itself, has an acquired immune deficiency syndrome. But there will always be some people in the Body whom we find we can cherish and be grateful for, with whatever patience we can muster. Friends, strangers, and sacraments: the communion of bodies and bread, all of us broken, all of us occasionally knowing new life breaking through our dying.

The last verse reminds us that it is only a narrow gate that leads to new life, to a spaciousness in which there is room to breathe, to a risen glory. The Law of Loving is relentless, fierce, tough. It insists we die to all possessiveness, all wealth, possessions, property, family, office, status, any and all substitutes for living with insecurity in faith. The image of a time of tribulation in the Book of Revelation is that of an olive press or wine press. We are the grapes: we go through the press to be become transformed into a wonderful vintage, about which we have no advance knowledge whatsoever.

Well, it is an affirmation of faith, but in difficult times, and tentatively expressed. It allows room for healthy doubt.

Prayers of Intercession

These are legion! This House Eucharist has two texts. Here is the first, followed by comment, then the second. This first one is adapted slightly from a litany by Thérèse Vanier of the L'Arche communities, and is reprinted with her permission.

That oppressed people
and those who oppress them
may free each other...

That those who are handicapped
and those who think they are not
may help each other...

That those who need someone to listen
may touch the hearts
of those who are too busy...

That the homeless
may bring joy to those
who open their doors reluctantly...

That the lonely
may heal those
who think they are self-sufficient...

That the poor
may melt the hearts
of the rich...

That seekers for truth
may give to those who are satisfied
they have found it...

That the dying
who do not want to die
may be comforted by those
who find it hard to live...

That the unloved
may be allowed to unlock the hearts
of those who cannot love...

That prisoners
may find true freedom
and liberate others from fear...

That those who sleep on the streets
may share their gentleness
with those who cannot understand them...

That the hungry
may tear the veil from the eyes
of those who do not hunger after justice...

That those who live without hope
may cleanse the hearts
of those who are afraid to live...

That the weak
may confound the strong
and save them...

That those who inflict hurt
may be bound by law
and transformed
by true and firm compassion...

That the cries of the violated
may be absorbed by the prayers
of the pain-bearers...

That those who are violent
may be overwhelmed by those
who are totally vulnerable...

That we may be healed...

Comment is superfluous, except to say that this prayer turns intercession on its head with the realization that those of us who come bearing gifts are often the ones most in need of receiving from the unlikely.

A practical point: the three dots after each of the prayers mean, Pause for a few moments to surround the intention with silent love. Resist the temptation to hurry on to the next. This is also a reminder that we should ideally take off our watches before a celebration of worship: on such occasions above all we are not to be governed by clock time. With due sensitivity, 'time out of time' does not go on for ever. With experience you know that some occasions will last a quarter of an hour or so, and some for three hours. The best party invitations do not say 'Carriages at eleven.'

Here is the alternative intercession, much more churchy!

Eternal and loving God,
in whose presence
we live the nights and days,
the darkness and the light,
by whose creative power
we are sustained,
we call to mind and heart
your world and your people,
that through our prayer
you would bless them.

Strengthen the worldwide
communion of churches,
that we may serve you
more faithfully.
Bless...
May those who confess your name
be united in your truth,
live together in your love,
and reveal your glory in the world.
Dear God, your will be done:
Your love be shown.

Bless and guide the powers that be,
give wisdom to all in authority,
to those who administer the law,
and to those who seek to reform it,
to the United Nations,
to the international courts of law
Bless...
Guide this and every land
in the ways of justice
and of peace,
that we may honour one another
and seek the common good.
Dear God, your will be done:
Your love be shown.

Give grace to us,
our families and friends,
to our neighbours,
to this parish,
and to all the people of this city.
Bless...
Give us a generous heart
to love as Christ loves us.
Dear God, your will be done:
Your love be shown.

Comfort and heal all those who suffer
the hurts of others' words and deeds,
the pains of flesh and feeling,
the bewilderments of dread and anxiety,
the despair of days and nights
without meaning.
Bless...
Give them courage and hope
in their troubles,
bring them the joy of your salvation,
and give to those who care for them
grace and skill to do your healing work.
Dear God, your will be done:
Your love be shown.

Hear us as we remember
those who have died,
whether in faith or doubt,
in trust or terror,
all whose deep desires
are known to you alone.
Bless...
Spread over them your peace
and healing grace,
and unite us with them
in your good time.
Dear God, your will be done:
Your love be shown.

Rejoicing in the fellowship of...
and of all the holy fools of God,
we commend ourselves
and all people
to your unfailing love.
Dear God, your will be done
throughout the universe:
Your love shine forth in glory.

Those familiar with the Alternative Service Book will recognize that this form is an adaptation of one of those in the Holy Communion Rite A. Because it is rather formal, we tend not to use it very much, preferring either the litany of Thérèse Vanier or simply a time of silent prayer punctuated by particular prayers from those who wish to voice them. But the occasional use of this more churchy form does serve as a reminder that to gather as a relatively small group in a home to celebrate the Eucharist is not the act of an independent sect. It may also serve to encourage lurking clergy to use this version on Sundays!

I find I can begin to make sense of intercession if I think of it, not as my attempt to persuade a distant God up there to act directly in the life of certain other people, rather as my willingness for whatever energy of love there is in my small being to be used as I seek to align it with the energy of God and 'imagine' it flowing into and through me towards others. I cannot prove that this is what happens, but I do believe that I myself become part of the praying and of whatever is happening in and through the praying. So it is that the opening prayer sets us all in the presence of the ever-creating and sustaining God: in and to that Presence we call to mind and heart those for whom we would pray, that *through* our prayer God will bless them.

If you recall that a blessing is the outpouring of abundant life and love, then I could not wish anything better for anyone. I would rather not presume to insist on an outcome of my prayer that I have decided beforehand, telling God that my will should be done: that you may be *blessed* is a more than sufficient intention. That is why the versicle and response at the end of each section is the hope that the will of God be done and the love of God be shown.

I also think that that general summing up of the particular prayers is a more mature way of asking for something than the more commonly used, Lord in your mercy, Hear our prayer; or Lord, hear my prayer, And let my cry come unto thee. I remain uneasy with the association of that language with the peasant petitioner pleading before King or Judge on bended knee–or the flunkey with exaggerated gesture of fluttering handkerchief, "We beseech thee to hear us, good Lord." No, we are called to grow in faith and love, to participate in the life of God, to be co-creators with God in the world. The language of our prayer needs to be consistent with human maturity.

I owe the phrase 'the worldwide communion of churches' to something Adrian Hastings wrote, alas I forget where. I recall that he used it as the most ecumenical and truly catholic phrase he could think of, hoping that the day would come when the whole Church *in* England would be one organic body within a worldwide communion of churches.

In the second section, I wanted to give equal weight to *both* law keepers *and* law reformers. The latter often get overlooked in 'established' prayers: I wonder why? And I think that the international bodies that seek peace and justice in a shrinking and fragile globe need all the help they can get.

I also think that the prayer for those who suffer needs balancing with the intention at the end of the fourth section, "and give to those who care for them grace (the divine) and skill (the human) to do your healing work."

In remembering in prayer those who have died, well, I have to come out of the closet and admit to universalist tendencies. In the generosity of Christ I find myself unable to give assent to a prayer limiting my intention to those who have died in Christ, and commending only ourselves and all *Christian* people to God's unfailing love (as it is written on p.125 of the ASB). I also believe that our prayers can touch those who have died in doubt or terror, especially those who have died suddenly, unexpectedly, or brutally. As web-tremblers of love, we would be rash to limit the effect of the 'ripples' to what we can sense in the current of this material, flesh-and-blood body.

Well, that has given enough room for considerable disagreement. All I would really say is that the words of our prayers do reflect our understanding of God, and that one generation's (or one individual's) particular forms don't necessarily get it completely right—neither a prayer supposedly hallowed by repetition over centuries, nor a prayer written today by those who rather assume that the world was created in the year in which they were born.

This time, the dots indicate places where specific names, places, and events can be contributed by anybody present. Something that exercises me as I write is the habit that most churches get into of mentioning by name only those in crisis. We seem more concerned about not forgetting the latest famine, conflict, or earthquake, and those in hospital or dying, than we do the everyday, the matter-of-fact, the largely taken for granted. It occurred to me only recently to be thankful in my prayers and to pray for John who runs the excellent fish and chip shop which I probably patronize more often than is good for me ('crazy prices' between six and nine, currently £1.20), or for the anonymous bus driver whose skill brought me safely home from the centre of town.

Perhaps, too, I could find room in my prayers for my love of islands. Yes, that's a task. By the time this book is in print, I hope to have added the name of a small(-ish) island for each day of the month. Thirty-one shouldn't be hard to find. When did you last pray for Tierra del Fuego or Stewart Island (the one falling off the southern cone of South America, the other off the south coast of the South Island of Aotearoa/New Zealand.) If I knew I wouldn't get my comeuppance I'd bet that that is the first time those islands have been mentioned in a book about or of prayers that has been written outside their specific neighbouring countries. I'd also be pretty sure that few people beyond geologists and whalers have given even a passing thought to South Georgia since the remnants of the imperial fleet recaptured it from the Argentinians in 1982, causing Mrs Thatcher in episcopal and regal style to bid us all 'rejoice'.

In case it is of interest or help, here is a list of prompts for specific prayers within each of the six sections above:

The churches:

> The ministry of leadership, ie in Anglican terms, bishops; vicars; associate, assistant, and apprentice vicars, commonly called curates; in Methodist terms, chair(men) of districts; superintendent ministers; circuit ministers.
>
> Other authorized ministers, both lay and ordained.
>
> Those discerning their future ministry and those beginning new ministries.
>
> Various churches, communities, associations, and networks.

The wider world

> The countries of the world
>
> The islands, oceans, wildernesses, river basins
>
> International concerns and organizations
>
> British concerns
>
> Writers and artists (Substitute teachers, scientists, etc. according to the concerns laid on your heart, as the Quakers would say.)

Our own particular patch

> Concerns of this city, town, village, neighbourhood
>
> Local people

Those in need

> Those living with HIV
>
> Those living with disabilities
>
> Those living with cancer
>
> Those who are anxious or depressed
>
> Those chronically unwell

Those in hospital

Those in prison

Those who are dying

Those who have died

Those who have died recently

Those whose anniversaries fall at this time

The saints

Greater, lesser, and local!

Praying in Christ

Abba, Amma, Beloved,
your name be hallowed,
your reign spread among us,
your will be done well,
at all times, in all places,
on earth as in heaven.
Give us the bread
we need for today.
Forgive us our trespass
as we forgive those
who trespass against us.
Let us not fail
in time of our testing.
Spare us from trials
too sharp to endure
Free us from the grip
of all evil powers.
For yours is the reign,
the power and the glory,
the victory of love,
for time and eternity,
world without end.
So be it. Amen.

The first two words are Aramaic, the language Jesus himself spoke. It seems that some people still have trouble with the notion of an inclusive fatherhood of God, inclusive in the old linguistic sense of the male gender being assumed to include the female. For us, the motherhood has actually to be stated. Hence Amma as well as Abba. They are of course both basic sound-words, among the first every infant learns and crossing many a boundary of culture and specific language.

It is notoriously difficult to translate the prayer that Luke and Matthew summed up as being particularly the way in which Jesus taught his disciples. The two versions differ in the Gospels, that of Matthew being the longer. All I have done here is to unfold the translations in a way which I hope has both dignity and rhythm.

In the traditional phrase 'Your kingdom come', the basic association is with a kind of rule rather than with geographical extent. Elsewhere I have used the word 'commonwealth' instead of 'kingdom', but I am not sure that the implication of God as a constitutional monarch is any more helpful than that of a medieval or oriental despot. We have also lost the sense of a covenant between ruler and people, with obligations on both sides. So I have chosen 'reign' here, aware of these difficulties of translation, and still searching for a phrase that could indicate something of the notion of a society where those who lead listen hard to everybody in their community or constituency, and seek to frame the rules and laws in a genuine attempt to express and enable the common good, with justice as the corporate embodiment of love. With the corruption of power so evident even in the best of human societies, we experience only faint approximations to life centred on the rule of God.

The fourth line used to say, "Your will be well done," but it sounded too much like an order for steak in a restaurant. So the last two words were reversed. In such small ways forms of worship evolve, as we become alert to the inevitability of changes of usage in a language. It all reminds me of a verse from the English Hymnal, in the long processional hymn, "Jerusalem my happy home". It reads thus:

> Our Lady sings Magnificat
> In tune surpassing sweet;
> And all the Virgins bear their parts,
> Sitting about her feet.

(EH 638, a sixteenth century translation of a Latin text of St Augustine.) I can't imagine the same translation being made – or used – today.

"Lead us not into temptation" was never a very good translation of the Greek 'peirasmos', which needs the sense of both 'test' and 'trial'. Hence two petitions rather than one: "Let us not fail in time of our testing," and "Spare us from trials too sharp to endure." 'Sharp' is a recent experiment, more vivid than my first attempt, which was simply 'too great to endure'. Sharper too!

I don't know about a personal being called the Devil. I do know a little of the power of evil. It is from evil's *grip* that I pray to be freed. from all manner of addictions and compulsions, any one of which can take over a person's life.

Lastly, so that the 'power' is not thought to be that of coercion and destruction, infecting both 'reign' and 'glory' I have added the line, "the victory of love", loyal to the most central conviction about God in the Scriptures.

And a footnote: In the Methodist form of the Holy Communion, the Lord's Prayer also comes at the end of the Intercessions, as a way of summing up our prayers. It seems to me that this is as appropriate a place as just before or after the sharing of bread and wine, with the association of "Give us this day our daily bread." It also leaves the act of communion less cluttered.

At the Taking of the Bread and Wine

> Blessed are you, eternal God,
> Source of all creation:
> through your goodness
> we have this bread to offer,
> which earth has given
> and human hands have made:
> it will become for us
> the Bread of Life.
> Blessed be God for ever.

Blessed are you, eternal God,
Source of all creation:
through your goodness
we have this wine to offer,
fruit of the vine
and work of human hands:
it will become for us
the Cup of Salvation.
Blessed be God for ever.

This prayer is basically from the Roman Catholic Missal, a contribution which has been valued and used by those of other traditions. "The Cup of Salvation" is a variant of "our spiritual drink".

The first two lines of each part have been changed from "Blessed are you, Lord, God of all creation", to avoid the complications of 'lordship' and to hint at the flowing energy that comes from an eternal source, the Spirit that animates and transforms.

Eucharistic Prayer

Two versions follow. No longer do the western churches have only one defining text, neither the Roman Canon nor the Prayer of Consecration in the Book of Common Prayer. Rather do we have a number of variations, held by a common intention. Broadly speaking, we offer gratitude ('eucharist') to God for creation and redemption in Christ, with particular emphases according to the day or season, and usually coming to a climax in the Sanctus (the outburst of praise which begins, "Holy, holy, holy.") There is a prayer to the Holy Spirit to transform the matter of bread and wine (and us), and an act of remembrance using the words from St Paul that tell us that the church was continually 'doing this' to re-member Jesus. I have used the hyphen deliberately. To re-member is to re-embody, to bring together, to bring alive, that which is of the past, and to make it effective in the present and for the future. And usually human hands touch both bread and cup. There is an act of memorial, i.e. a recollection that we are participating in the one great sacrifice of the death and resurrection of Christ, and making our own sacrifice of praise and thanksgiving.

The Book of Common Prayer of the Episcopal Church of the United States (1976) has this guidance in the version of the Great Thanksgiving where the text is not printed out in full:

"The Celebrant gives thanks to God the Father for his work in creation and his revelation of himself to his people; recalls before God, when appropriate, the particular occasion being cele-brated; incorporates or adapts the Proper Preface of the day, if desired. (NB 'Proper' means 'Special' not the opposite of 'Improper', and 'Preface' is 'that which comes before' the Sanctus.) If the Sanctus is to be included, it is introduced with these or similar words... The Celebrant now praises God for the salvation of the world through Jesus Christ our Lord. The Prayer continues with these words (a prayer to the Holy Spirit is printed). At the following words concerning the bread, the Celebrant is to hold it, or lay a hand upon it; and at the words concerning the cup, to hold or place a hand upon the cup and any other vessel containing wine to be consecrated. (The actual text follows.)"

Eucharistic Prayer 1

The God of Love
is in the midst of us:
The Holy Spirit
dwells among us.

We surrender our hearts
to our faithful Creator:
We open them to God
and to one another.

Let us give thanks
to the Living Mystery:
With joy and delight
we give praise.

Let us give thanks
for the wonder of God's glory,
for the gift of this our planet,

beautiful and fragile in the heavens,
for our responsibility as guardians
of all that is being created,
for the vision of one human commonwealth
with peace known on earth
and goodwill shared among all people.

Drawn by the magnet of the living God
ever closer to the Presence of the Mystery,
We adore the God who gives us life.

Let us give thanks for Jesus of Nazareth,
living the truth of us and the truth of God,
glad to be born of Mary to dwell with us,
a man most gloriously alive,
yet enduring to the end and dying
as the means of our reconciliation
and our healing,
who is most awesomely risen,
the pioneer of our salvation.
Drawn by the magnet of the suffering God
ever closer to the Presence of the Mystery,
We praise the Christ
who bears our pain and makes us whole.

Let us give thanks for the Holy Spirit,
moving invisibly deep within us,
spinning the thread of attention among us,
bringing to life in us
the Way and Wisdom of Jesus,
nurturing us with the food of the living God,
and with the fountain of water
that wells up to eternal life,
sending us into the heart
of the conflicts of the world,
to speak the words and live the lives
of justice and of peace,
of truth and of healing,
and so become transformed
by the yearning cry of God.

Drawn by the magnet of the loving God
ever closer to the Presence of the Mystery,
We give thanks for the Spirit
who makes love with us
in the dance of the new creation.

So let us give thanks to God
for accepting us in the Beloved,
who in the night of loneliness and desolation,
of agony and betrayal,
took the bread that sustains us all,
gave thanks, and broke it,
and gave it to his disciples and said,

Take, eat, this is my Body,
my Living Presence, given for you:
do this to re-member me,
to bring us together in the world.

In the same way he took the cup of wine,
the wine of our sorrow and our solace,
gave thanks, and gave it to them and said,

Drink of this, all of you,
this is my Blood,
my Very Life, spent for you:
do this to re-member me,
to bring us alive in the world.

[Silence]

Creator Spirit,
as we celebrate the one great sacrifice of love,
hover now over your people,
over this bread and wine,
that they may be to us
the Body and Blood of Christ.
For in the mystery of faith,

Christ has died,
Christ is risen,

Christ is here,
Christ will come.

And now with all who have ever lived,
with saints and martyrs
and forgotten faithful people,
with angels and archangels
and all the heavenly company,
with all who are alive
and all who are yet to be born,
with all creation in all time,
with joy we sing:

Holy! Holy! Holy!
Beating Heart of Glory,
All your works shall praise your name
In earth and sky and sea!
Holy! Holy! Holy!
Strong in Love and Mercy,
God in Three Persons,
Blessed Trinity!

Blessed is the One who comes
in the Name of our God!
Hosanna in the Highest!

Alleluia! Alleluia!
Praise to the God of Splendour!
So be it! Amen!

A few comments. Two bishops of the Church of England first brought to my attention two of the images used here, the 'magnet' that is God drawing us close by the very attractiveness of love (Alec Graham, the present Bishop of Newcastle in a sermon twenty-five years ago), and the picture of the Holy Spirit 'spinning the thread of attention' (John V. Taylor, the former Bishop of Winchester, in his book *The Go-Between God*, SCM Press, 1972). That is a glimpse into the process of shaping prayers in the organism that is the Body of Christ. It may be that the two images are original to the two bishops, but they were used by them in an attempt to communicate something of the Gospel in the twentieth century. I don't know if they themselves have ever used them in saying a eucharistic prayer, but they might well have done if they had been bishops in the early centuries, who usually extemporized the whole prayer. Indeed, the 'threads' sewing us all together through space and time are often unknown, often subtle in their transmission, but nevertheless witnessing to the richness of the Great Tradition (or the Great Momentum as George Guiver puts it in his book *Faith in Momentum*, SPCK, 1990).

In the three sections that begin, "Drawn by...", there is adoration, praise, thanks, words that are interchangeable; God the Trinity is addressed, the life-giver, pain-bearer, love-maker, the living, suffering, loving God, who draws us into the Dance, the ever-moving, energetic, creating, mysterious Presence.

The acclamation of faith is usually "Christ has died, Christ is risen, Christ will come again." It occurred to me that we are celebrating the *presence* of Christ among us through bread and wine, so that the line "Christ is here" is particularly appropriate. Also, the manner of any future coming(s) is not dependent on the old picture of an appearance in the clouds at the end of the world. As a matter of historical fact, he did not 'come again' in the way the early Christians expected within their generation. Better then to say, "Christ will come" and leave the manner open. Or maybe, "Christ will come again—and again."

The Sanctus is in the form of a re-working of a verse of the hymn, *Holy, holy, holy, Lord God Almighty,* and is followed by the Benedictus. Looking at the prayer as a whole, the volume of sound, as it were, is medium at the beginning, becomes quieter until the period of silence, and then rises to its crescendo. Again, there is nothing uniquely right about this, but it seems to work in practice as an alternative rhythm to others that are on offer.

Eucharistic Prayer 2

> Let us contemplate in wonder,
> awe, and gratitude
> the universe of which we are a part,
> the vast expanse of interstellar space,
> galaxies, suns, the planets in their courses,

and this beautiful and fragile earth,
our island home.

[Silence]

Let us with dignified humility
accept our vocation
to be trustees of all that lives
and breathes under the sun,
to be skilful in probing
the mysteries of creation,
to be wise and reverent in our use
of the resources of the earth.

[Silence]

So let us greet the God
who is within us and beyond us:
Creator Spirit, Energy Inspiring,
brooding over the formless deeps,
wings outstretched in the primal dark,
enclosing and calling forth
all that has come to be,
ever present to renew and re-create,

beckoning all that is chaotic
and without form—
the spontaneous leap
of microscopic particles,
the isolated impulse
of the human heart—
weaving them into the pattern
of a larger whole,

urging forward into ever more complex
forms of life,
planting an awareness and faint yearning
for the unattained,

challenging a choosing
of the unknown yet to be,
a risk that is a dying

that a fuller life be born,
a sacrifice of lesser ways,
a giving up of slaughter,
the law of gentleness
in the midst of force and fury,

a way made known to us
by Jesus of Nazareth,
eternal persuasive love
made visible at last,
the love that through the aeons
of unrecorded time
has striven and suffered,
died and risen to new life,
within the very fabric of the universe,
accepting us so deeply
that we need no longer seize and possess
out of malice and of fear,
clearing the way for us to be empowered
to mend creation's threads
that we have torn,
to make the desert bloom
and the trees to grow again
on barren ground.

[Silence]

So we take the produce of this earth,
the bread of our sustenance,
the wine of our solace and our sorrow,
as Jesus commanded us to do,
that we might know Creator Spirit
transfiguring our flesh and blood
to a glory that we but dimly sense,
filling us with the living presence,
the very self, of Jesus,
given, sacrificed for us,
to bring us alive,
to bring us together as one body.

For he took bread, gave thanks, broke it,
and gave it to his disciples and said,
Take, eat, this is my Body
which is given for you;
do this to re-member me.

In the same way, after supper,
he took a cup of wine, gave thanks,
and gave it to them and said,
Drink of this, all of you,
this is my Blood of the new covenant,
which is shed for you and for many
for the forgiveness of sins:
do this, as often as you drink it,
to re-member me.

Creator Spirit, as we celebrate
the one great sacrifice of love,
hover now over your people,
over this bread and wine,
that they may be to us
the Body and Blood of Christ,
for in the mystery of faith,

Christ has died,
Christ is risen,
Christ is here,
Christ will come.

Through Christ, with Christ, in Christ,
by the power and in the presence
of Creator Spirit,
with all that lives throughout the universe,
seen and unseen,
we worship you, eternal God of Love,
in songs of everlasting praise:

Holy! Holy! Holy!
Beating Heart of Glory!
All your works shall praise your Name
In earth and sky and sea!

Holy! Holy! Holy!
Strong in Love and Mercy!
God in Three Persons,
Blessed Trinity!

Blessed is the One who comes
in the Name of our God
Hosanna in the Highest!

Alleluia! Alleluia!
Praise to the God of Splendour!
So be it! Amen!

This particular prayer was written in response to an invitation
from a church which was putting together a special service on
the theme of creation. The first section, beginning, "Let us
contemplate...", is derived from one of the eucharistic prayers of
the Episcopal Church of the United States. I think the second
section, beginning, "Let us with dignified humility..." is original.
It attempts to be positive about the contributions that science
and technology can make at their best to the common good.

The longer third section, beginning, "So let us greet the God
who is within us and beyond us...", relies heavily on the first
chapter of John Taylor's *The Go-Between God*. In it he seeks to give
a theological interpretation of the understanding of the ways the
universe works that is being shown to us by contemporary sci-
entists—the patterns, complexities, and risks that seem to be part
of the evolving fabric of life. Love is a late arrival on the scene,
but is focused on its embodiment in Jesus.

There are echoes, too, of Genesis (the Spirit brooding over the
formless deeps) and of Isaiah (the hope of the barren once more
becoming fertile).

The Breaking of the Bread

The bread which we break
is a sharing in the Body of Christ.
The wine which we bless
is a sharing in the Blood of Christ.

These words are commonly used at this point of the service. It would be hard to improve on them, though of course there are other possibilities.

Agnus Dei

> Lamb of God,
> taking away the sin of the world,
> having compassion upon us:
> Beloved of God,
> affirming the worth of the world,
> accepting us in love for ever:
> Healing God,
> bearing the pain of the world,
> giving us and all creation your peace:
> Pour mercy upon us,
> whisper your love for us,
> give us peace.

This is a new unfolding of the traditional Agnus Dei. In the Arctic, 'seal' would be substituted for 'lamb', the latter being completely unknown there.

I owe the word 'pour' to Simon Bailey. In his poetic sensitivity he reckoned that the phrase "*Pour* mercy upon us" was more vivid than the usual "*Have* mercy upon us." The association could be with the oil of anointing or with the water of cleansing and refreshment.

After saying these words, we sing the last phrase in Latin, "Dona nobis pacem." It can be sung in a round, and I am told that the melody was composed by Mozart, though I have not been able to track it down. It is printed in the handy script for group use of all these texts and available by following the instructions which you will find in the Preface on page v.

Invitation to Communion

> Let us open our hands,
> open our hearts,
> open the hidden places
> of our being,

and into our deep soul-self
let there enter the heartbeat
of those we love,
the lifeblood of our villages,
towns, and cities,
the lifestream of the tides
and currents and seasons,
the pulsing of our planet
and of the stars;
let there enter all the joys and pains
our cup can bear,
let us be nourished by the new life
that comes through what is broken;
and in and through it all,
to transform it to glory,
let us receive the Body,
the Living Presence,
the Blood, the Very Self,
of Jesus,
and let us feed and live and love,
in faith, with gratitude.

Beloved, we draw near to be loved by you,
in deep yet trembling trust,
through this matter of your creation,
this material stuff of bread and body,
this fluid of wine and blood,
that your desire for us and ours for you
may be blended in deep joy and ecstasy,
that we may be enriched and doubly blessed.

We draw near to receive
this offering of yourself,
your intimate, vulnerable,
and naked body,
imparted to us,
incorporated in us,
that we may dwell and love
and create,
you in us and we in you.

The first section of this invitation was written overlooking the
turbulent currents of the narrow strip of water between Bardsey
Island and the mainland of Wales. Again, associations of a
particular place and a particular tradition are brought into the
celebration.

The second section brings associations of sexuality into the
prayer, sadly lacking in most liturgies. After all, this is an act of
love and communion in which we are participating, and we need
to combine boldness with sensitivity in suggesting that it might
not be accidental to associate the sexual with the spiritual. It is
not accidental either if you catch a hint of the ironies of the
mingling of bodily fluids, which can give new life or be the
harbinger of a new and particularly cruel death.

Those familiar with the cadences of the Book of Common
Prayer may, in the third section, catch an echo of the Prayer of
Humble Access, without the suspicion of flesh and blood implicit
in "...that our sinful bodies may be made clean by his Body, and
our souls washed through his most precious Blood," yet with the
words from the Fourth Gospel, "...and that we may evermore
dwell in him, and he in us."

A Roman Catholic priest friend of mine told me that it was a
custom in the early days of the Church to respond at communion with the words "I am" when given the consecrated
bread with the words "The Body of Christ". We sometimes do
this: it can be an awesome and glorious moment.

After Communion

> Ever-loving and ever-creating God,
> feeding us with Living Bread,
> delighting us with the Wine of New Life,
> giving us a pledge of unbounded Love,
> celebrating with us
> the dawn of a new creation,
> joining us to one another
> in the Mystical Body of Christ,
> we give you thanks and praise,
> we offer you ourselves,
> all that we have

and all that we are,
and we yearn with eager longing
for the fulfilment of all things in Christ,
Alpha and Omega,
our Beginning and our End.

This prayer is simply an attempt to re-work the thanksgiving after communion in the Book of Common Prayer. I think the original is a very good one, but I now reckon (after some disasters) that it is unhelpful merely to tinker with a few words of an old prayer. So this new prayer takes up the same themes and expresses them in a different way.

A song of blessing

Refrain: Sing of your love, now and for ever.

O God of our ancestors' faith, we bless you...
We bless your holy and glorious name...
We bless you on the heights of the mountains...
We bless you in deep and secret places...
We bless you in songs of animals and birds...
We bless you in the sounds of the city...
We bless you in the bread and the wine...
We bless you in the Body and the Blood...

This is a canticle similar to quite a few others, and can be sung to any simple chant. An example is included in the collection of these texts referred to above and described in the Preface. Sometimes we substitute a hymn special to the day or season.

The Blessing

The Blessing of God be with us,
Father and Mother
Sustainer of our earth,
Source of all that is
and that shall be.

The Blessing of God be with us,
the Messiah, the Christ,
the Risen and Glorious Loved One
and our Friend.

The Blessing of God be with us,
Spirit spreading love and joy
in our hearts,
giving hope to the battered ones,
inspiring justice and peace
for the little ones.

May this rich blessing be with us,
with all humankind
living and departed,
and with all the creatures
of land and sea and air.
May our days be long
on this good earth.

For we have been nourished
by the Bread of Life,
we have been quickened
by the Lifeblood of the Universe.
With courage and in hope
let us continue on the journey.

Amen. Thanks be to God.

Again, this is but one of many appropriate blessings. It is sometimes followed by music, sometimes by silence, especially in winter with the lights turned off and the candlelight flickering, and the streetlamps of the city seen clearly through the window. More often there is an informal greeting of Peace and Blessing, more individual and personal than the prayerful greeting near the beginning. Holiness embraces a hubbub!

4

The Feast of Fools:
Sample of a Special Context

HERE is a sample of some special material to help celebrate the
First of April, bearing in mind the tradition of the Holy Fool, the
Clown who takes the worst and bounces back for more, and the
Jester who has no power but has licence to tell the King the
truth.

The first section of the Approach builds on words of St Paul,
the second and third sections are taken from my book *Prayer at
Night*, as amended during the course of a revision for a fifth
edition due sometime in 1997.

After saying the words of the Dedication we pass round,
neighbour to neighbour, a harlequin hat which a friend of mine
made for me some years ago, each placing the hat on the head of
the person next to them and saying the words, "Be a fool, for
Christ's sake."

Approach

> Fools to the world,
> we know the wisdom of God.
> Unknown, we cannot be ignored.
> Dying, we still live on.
> Disciplined by suffering,
> we are not beaten down.
> Knowing sorrow,
> we have always cause for joy.
> Poor ourselves, we make many rich.
> Penniless, we own the world.
> Steadfastly we turn our wills towards God,
> to meet hardships and afflictions,
> hunger and weariness, illness and failure,
> with sincerity, insight, patience, kindness,
> speaking the truth in love,
> resilient in the power of the Spirit.

We have injured your love:
Binder of wounds, heal us.
We stumble in the darkness:
Light of the world, guide us.
We forget that we are your home:
Spirit of God, dwell in us.

God of Joy, we rejoice in you.
You run to meet us like a welcoming friend,
you laugh with us in the merriment of heaven,
you feast with us at the great banquet,
Clown of clowns, Fool of fools,
the only Entertainer of jesters.
God of Joy, we rejoice in you.

Readings

1 Corinthians 1.18-31

Mark 10.32-45

From *The Feast of Fools* by Harvey Cox

One of the earliest representations of Christ in
Christian art depicts a crucified human figure with
the head of an ass. For years experts have disputed
about what it means. Some think it may be a secret
sign, others a cruel parody. Either could be the case.
But it might also be true that those catacomb
Christians had a deeper sense of the comic ab-
surdity of their position that we think they did. A
wretched band of slaves, derelicts, and square pegs,
they must have sensed occasionally how ludicrous
their claims appeared. They knew they were 'fools
for Christ', but also claimed that the foolishness of
God is wiser than human wisdom. Christ himself
for them must have been something of a holy fool.

Furthermore, even in the biblical portrait of
Christ there are elements that suggest clown symbols. Like the jester, Christ defies custom and scorns
crowned heads. Like a wandering troubadour he

has no place to lay his head. Like the clown in the circus parade, he satirizes existing authority by riding into town replete with regal pageantry when he has no earthly power. Like a minstrel he frequents dinner parties. At the end he is costumed by his enemies in a mocking caricature of royal paraphernalia. He is crucified amidst sniggers and taunts with a sign over his head that lampoons his laughable claims.

Dedication

Let us be fools for Christ's sake:
In facing the truth,
may we be set free from illusion.
In accepting our wounds,
may we be healed.
In embracing the outcast,
may we be redeemed.
In discovering our child,
may we grow to maturity.
In seeking true innocence,
may we no longer harm.
In yielding to dying,
may abundant life flow into us.
In vulnerable risk,
may we know love's pain and joy.
In the release of laughter,
may we hear the chuckle of God.
In the folly of the Cross,
may we see the Wisdom of God.

Hymn

[The words are by Brian Wren. The tune 'Shrub End' by Peter Cutts was composed for this hymn and can be found in several books. Alternatively, 'Knecht' is suitable.]

Here hangs a man discarded,
a scarecrow hoisted high,
a nonsense pointing nowhere
to all who hurry by.

Can such a clown of sorrows
still bring a useful word
when faith and love seem phantoms
and every hope absurd?

Yet there is help and comfort
for lives by comfort bound,
when drums of dazzling progress
give strangely empty sound.

Life, emptied of all meaning,
drained out in bleak distress,
can share in broken silence
our deepest emptiness;

And love that freely enters
the pit of life's despair
can name our hidden darkness
and suffer with us there.

Christ, in our darkness risen,
help all who long for light
to hold the hand of promise
till faith receives its sight.

5
For Easter:
Another sample of a special context

THE first part of the service merely hints at a confession of sins, appropriate after Lent! "Christos aneste!" and "Christos voskrese!" are Greek and Russian respectively for "Christ is risen!" The next two sections are slightly amended from Eric Milner-White's book, *My God, My Glory*. The hymn that follows is a variant on *Jesus Christ is risen today*, and can be sung to the same tune.

The hymn *Sing choirs of God* can be sung to the tune *Woodlands*. It is based on one that can be found in *Lent, Holy Week, and Easter*, published by Church House Publishing (1984, 1986), but it has been considerably re-worked. (The original is in fact a metrical version of the beginning of the Exultet, the Easter Song of Praise, a medieval prose-poem often sung during the Easter Vigil.)

Alleluias

> Christos aneste!
> Christos voskrese!
> Alleluia!
> Christ is risen indeed!
> Alleluia!
>
> You are risen, O Christ.
> Let the gospel trumpets speak
> and the news, as of holy fire,
> burning and flaming and inextinguishable,
> run to the ends of the earth.
> Alleluia! Alleluia!
> You are risen, O Christ.
> Let all creation greet the good news
> with jubilant shout,
> for its redemption has come,

the long night is past,
the Saviour lives,
and rides and reigns in triumph,
now and to the ages of ages.
Alleluia! Alleluia!

Christ once crucified now lives, Alleluia!
Blessedness to all he gives, Alleluia!
Laughter echoes round the earth, Alleluia!
Grief gives way to joy and mirth, Alleluia!

Hell no longer holds us fast, Alleluia!
Fate has loosed its grip at last, Alleluia!
Love has melted every fear, Alleluia!
Death proves kindly, Christ is near, Alleluia!

Celebrate this joyful feast, Alleluia!
People all, the greatest least, Alleluia!
Drop your masks of pomp and pride, Alleluia!
Greet the Clown with wounded side, Alleluia!

The glory of the risen Christ
shrivels up our pride!
The power of the risen Christ
sets us free from evil's grip!
The touch of the risen Christ
heals our deepest wounds and sorrow!
The life of the risen Christ
swallows up our fear of death!
Alleluia! Alleluia!

We are indeed healed,
forgiven, embraced in love,
set free to live
in the Spirit of the Risen Christ.

The Peace of the Risen Christ
spread among us.
Alleluia!

Prayers

O Christ, radiant Light,
shining in our darkness,
most glorious of the children of earth,
Holy One setting captives free:
Christ of the living God,
give freedom to the peoples of the world.

O Christ, stooping low in great humility,
obedient to death,
walking the way of the cross,
calling us to follow
to death and to resurrection:
Christ of the living God,
keep your people faithful to your way.

O Christ, casting out
the fear that holds us back
from one another,
melting all that freezes
and keeps us cold:
Christ of the living God,
give us the gifts of friendship.

O Christ, saving us in our poverty,
reconciling us
to the Source of all that is,
making us a holy people,
a commonwealth,
and priests to our God:
Christ of the living God,
bring new life and hope
in the midst of human pain.

O Christ, showering us with generous gifts,
saving us from the fear of death,
giving us a share in your life:
Christ of the living God,
cause us to walk with confidence
the waters of our dying.

At the taking of the bread and wine

O God of our ancestors,
blessed be your name for ever.
Yours is the greatness, the power, the glory,
the splendour, and the majesty.
For everything in the heavens
and on the earth is yours.

From your hand
come all the blessings of life,
open gifts of goods and honour,
secret gifts in pain and dying.
Even in the midst of change and decay,
O God, you reign for ever and ever,
pouring out your life in love for us,
even to weakness,
to emptiness and dread,
yearning for us to respond,
drawing us closer to your presence.

And so we give you thanks, O God,
and praise your glorious name,
for all things come from you,
and of your own do we give you.

The last part of the Eucharistic Prayer

[After the proclaiming of the mystery of faith]

Come, Holy and Mysterious Spirit
of the Risen Christ;
Come, Love Divine,
Heartbeat of the Universe;
Come, True Vine and Living Bread,
Resurrection and Eternal Life;
Come, Paschal Lamb,
Slaughtered Victim,
Helpless and Vulnerable Lover,
Living Sacrifice,
Lifeblood of the Universe;

Come, Christ of Pain,
dying, descending to the depths
to face all hell let loose,
and meeting there the Joy
that redeems all tragedy and all loss;
Come, Risen Christ,
with glorious wounds to touch
and heal and forgive;
Come, Life-giving Spirit,
Bearer of the Risen Christ
to us in this bread and wine;
Come, Spirit of Easter Fire,
transfigure this thanksgiving meal
into the food of the pilgrim people,
sustaining us with Christ's Body
and Christ's Blood;
Come, now and at the end of time,
and spread the Easter Banquet
of our salvation.

Dying, you destroyed our death!
rising, you restored our life!
living Christ, come in glory!
Alleluia! Alleluia!

And now, with all who have ever lived,
with saints and martyrs
and forgotten faithful people,
with angels and archangels
and all the heavenly company,
with all who are alive
and all who are yet to be born,
with all creation in all time,
with joy we give praise:

Holy, holy, holy,
eternal God of Power and Love,
all space and all time
show forth your glory,
Alleluia! Amen!

Sing, choirs of God, let saints and angels sing,
the universe exult in harmony.
We greet you, Christ, now risen from the grave,
And join our voices to the symphony.

Sing, choirs of God, behold your light has come;
The glorious wounds of Christ shine full and clear.
We lift our hearts for love has conquered pain,
The night is gone, the dawn at last is here.

Sing, choirs of God, exult in joy outpoured,
The gospel trumpet tell of victory won.
Dear Christ, you live, and love us to the end,
We shout with all the world the long Amen.

The Easter Anthems

We praise you, O Christ,
risen from the dead,
breaking death's dominion,
rising from the grave.

Absorbing in yourself
the force of evil's ways,
you destroyed death's age-old sting
and now you are alive for evermore.

Let us find our life in you
breaking through our fear of everlasting void.
For you are risen from the dead,
the first fruits of those who sleep.

From the days of first awareness
we betrayed the call of life,
yet yearned for that communion
which still we dimly sense.

Pain and evil, malice and cruel greed,
these deepened the sorrow of our hearts.
Yet they are done away in light of glorious dawn,
the victory of resurrection day.

At one with all who've lived,
so all of us have died,
at one with your humanity,
all shall be made alive.

Hymn

[The words are by Brian Wren. The tune 'Jackson New' was composed by William P. Rowan and is printed in *Praising a Mystery*, Hope Publishing Company, distributed in the UK by Stainer & Bell Ltd. Other tunes to the metre 8.7.8.7.D will also serve.]

Christ is risen! Shout Hosanna!
Celebrate this day of days!
Christ is risen! Hush in wonder:
all creation is amazed.
In the desert all-surrounding,
see, a spreading tree has grown.
Healing leaves of grace abounding
bring a taste of love unknown.

Christ is risen! Raise your spirits
from the caverns of despair.
Walk with gladness in the morning,
see what love can do and dare.
Drink the wine of resurrection,
not a servant, but a friend.
Jesus is our strong companion.
Joy and peace shall never end.

Christ is risen! Earth and heaven
nevermore shall be the same.
Break the bread of new creation
where the world is still in pain.
Tell its grim, demonic chorus:
"Christ is risen! Get you gone!"
God the First and Last is with us.
Sing Hosanna everyone!